IMAGES OF ENGLAND

CAMBRIDGE

IMAGES OF ENGLAND

CAMBRIDGE

SUE SLACK

TEMPUS

Frontispiece: The Central Library Reading Room, *c.* 1930. The library was located in this magnificent domed room in the Guildhall building, which is now the Tourist Information Office, between 1862 and 1975, when it moved into Lion Yard. Cambridge Central Library this year celebrates 150 years of library service in Cambridge; it was begun in 1855 by Borough Librarian John Pink.

First published 2005

Tempus Publishing Limited
The Mill, Brimscombe Port,
Stroud, Gloucestershire, GL5 2QG
www.tempus-publishing.com

British Library Cataloguing in Publication Data.
A catalogue record for this book is available from the British Library.

ISBN 0 7524 3623 6

Typesetting and origination by Tempus Publishing Limited.
Printed in Great Britain.

Contents

A policeman pauses, on Market Hill, during his busy beat to be photographed with market traders and shoppers, with the tower of Great St Mary's in the background.

Acknowledgements

The author wishes to thank Cambridgeshire Libraries, Archives and Information for providing the photographs, the editor of the *Cambridge Evening News* for allowing the use of some of his photographs and grateful thanks to Chris Jakes for the introduction and for his useful criticism.

Special thanks to those who have deposited material with the Cambridgeshire Collection, without whom this book would not have been possible. The Collection always welcomes any donations of any additional material.

Introduction

Cambridge is a place that means something to most people. They will have heard of the name, often alongside its older rival Oxford, and if they have not been one of the millions of visitors who have seen the city for themselves, then they will imagine a city made up entirely of ancient college courts, lush lawns, students in gowns, choristers from King's, with punts and rowing crews moving effortlessly on the river.

These, however, are images drawn from only one part of the story of Cambridge. The university began life almost 800 years ago when scholars fleeing Oxford made their home in the small provincial county town of Cambridge that, as a result, would become world famous. The relationship between the town and the university has not been without its difficulties over the years, featuring both riots and rags, with each side keen to defend and extend their privileges and position at the expense of the other.

This volume, for the most part, shows the reality of town rather than gown life: the streets where people lived and worked and the shops where the everyday necessities of life could be bought. It shows Cambridge people at work and the transport they used to get to work and also to escape from it on holidays. It shows Cambridge people at play and the inns where they went to socialise, relax and enjoy themselves, and one where, because this is Cambridge, two future Nobel Prize winners announced to the world that they had discovered the secret of life. The effects of two world wars on the town and university are shown. The First World War saw Cambridge used as a mobilisation centre, with thousands of soldiers gathering here before leaving for France, and only too swiftly saw many returning wounded to the large military hospital established here. The role women played in the war is shown and while this resulted in them eventually being given the vote, the university would wait even longer to award them equal status to men. The colleges emptied of students again in the Second World War and as the young men and women and their tutors went off to fight, to work as codebreakers and to construct the atomic bomb, Cambridge itself suffered as a result of enemy action. The river from which Cambridge takes its name is shown as both commercial artery and leisure playground, and a magnet for the photographer.

The photographs in this volume are taken from the illustrations archive held in the Cambridgeshire Collection, the local studies department of Cambridge Central Library, which holds more than 400,000 images and negatives dating from the seventeenth century to the present day, depicting all aspects of life in the city, university and county of Cambridge. It is fitting that this volume is published in the year we celebrate the 150th anniversary of the public library in Cambridge and of the creation of the Cambridgeshire Collection by our first librarian, John Pink. The first library building opened on 28 June 1855 and from the very beginning the stock included books and pamphlets relating to Cambridge and its people. The Cambridgeshire Collection today exists to collect, organise and make available to the public an extraordinary wealth and range of material reflecting the past, present and future of our county, and relies to a large extent on the support and generosity of people who enjoy using the collection and wish to share their own work and material with others.

They will enjoy seeing this selection of photographs of Cambridge, many of which have not been previously published. As, I am sure, will all those who have spent part of their lives living, working or studying in the city, and the many new visitors who will perhaps now take away a broader view of the history of this truly unforgettable city.

Chris Jakes
County Local Studies Librarian
Cambridgeshire Collection
May 2005

one

Inns

Cambridge has always had a great number of inns and public houses to serve thirsty academia and all its ancillary workers, as well as the inhabitants of the city after their daily work. It was also on the route of coaches from London and other major cities and so had many coaching inns with stables and rooms for travellers.

Inns served many other functions apart from the obvious one of providing drink and hospitality. In the absence of public rooms, inns were used as coroner's offices and election offices, and soldiers were often billeted there too. All manner of political and social meetings were held in the public rooms and they were centres of entertainment, sport and music. The coaching inns would receive news and newspapers from London, so would be the news centres of the town, and doctors would even meet their patients there, in the absence of surgeries within the residential area of their patients. They therefore provided a valuable service to the community, although not everyone thought so.

A register of Soldiers' Billets taken in the late nineteenth century named no fewer than 470 taverns in the town that were compelled to house soldiers. At that time, there were some thirty in Newmarket Road alone. A social survey of 1904 expressed concern that in the same street there were pubs every 36 yards, in a street measuring 796 yards, and that in Castle Street there were no fewer than eleven inns in total. This is not as worrying as it sounds. Drinking beer was actually much healthier than drinking water at the time, as the water was polluted and dangerous until cleansing measures improved the water supply. The atmosphere of the pub was also very attractive to those who lived in poor housing with little heat and light and provided company, mainly for men, at the end of the day. The women who frequented the inns and taverns were usually of easy virtue and gambling, cockfights and bear-baiting have all been recorded in Cambridge inns in the past.

Many of the ancient inns have disappeared; these are a few that have gone and some that have survived.

The Wrestlers Inn, situated at the corner of Petty Cury and St Andrew's Street, was once one of the city's finest Jacobean buildings with its timber beams, oriel windows, and rich carving, its gaily painted plasterwork and its pargeting of Tudor roses. However, by the end of nineteenth century it had become shabby and in need of repair. Records show that its courtyard had been used as a fencing ground in the 1850s and that bear-baiting had also taken place there in 1749. At one time it had been used as a customs office and as a soldiers' billet between 1841-64. The inn was sold in 1875 to Robert Sayle the draper for £5,250 and demolished in 1883 to provide the site for the old post office at the entrance to Petty Cury. This picture was taken in around 1880, before the inn's demolition. The area again came under the bulldozer in 1972 when the Lion Yard was built. A pub in Newmarket Road later took its name.

The Falcon. An inn had stood on this site off Petty Cury since 1504, when Richard King of Wisbech gave the land to the Prior of Barnwell. Elizabeth I is said to have stayed here in one of the galleries which made the Falcon the largest galleried inn in Cambridge. Plays were performed here, with the gentry seated in the galleries and the poor standing in the courtyard below. In the eighteenth century, the east side was converted into assembly rooms while the other side remained open until 1820. The yard then became an overcrowded slum with around 300 people sharing just two privies. One house contained thirteen families, sometimes seven people to a room. The whole area was condemned by the Medical Officer of Health in 1885 and demolished in 1903, shortly after this photograph was taken.

The Red Lion, one of a number of inns which served the market area of Cambridge, was another inn that was situated in Petty Cury. Rebuilt in the eighteenth century as a large coaching inn, when travel became more extensive, it managed to survive the advent of the railway in 1845, when many smaller yards were lost. It had its own horse-bus to take travellers to and from the station and had large assembly rooms which catered for the local gentry, who held balls and dinners there. It was the only Petty Cury inn to survive beyond 1900 but it was demolished in 1969, later giving its name to the Lion Yard shopping precinct. This photograph shows the inn at the time of the county elections in 1874, festooned with election posters for the Conservative candidate Francis Sharp Powell.

The Bun Shop, seen here decorated for the Coronation in 1953, survived until the 1970s. It was situated at St Andrew's Hill, Downing Street. A popular pub, which was often mentioned in the *Good Beer Guide*, it could not resist the tide of progress and was demolished after 1974. Its name was taken by a pub in King Street in 1992.

The Bird Bolt Hotel, *c.* 1870. This inn stood at the corner of St Andrew's Street and Downing Street and got its name from the bolt or arrow which was shot from a crossbow used in hunting. An inn had stood on this site for hundreds of years. In 1835 it was a commercial hotel; by 1876 it had billiard rooms; by 1891 it was listed as a Temperance Hotel and shops were later added on the ground floor. The inn was demolished in around 1970. It was on the site of the Norwich Union building which itself has recently been demolished to make way for the Grand Arcade development in the centre of Cambridge.

The White Horse Inn, *c.* 1930. Still standing on the corner of Castle Street and Northampton Street and now home to the Folk Museum, the White Horse was a sixteenth-century inn that was open until 1934. Recently reopened after a major refurbishment, this museum holds many items relating to the social history of Cambridge.

The Three Tuns was built in the seventeenth century. This ancient inn was said to be the haunt of the highwayman Dick Turpin. Legend has it that, unable to settle his bill one day and needing to get away fast, he left his jacket in lieu of payment; the landlord would not have been too cross, as the pockets revealed a handful of costly jewels! This inn stood where Bell's Court on Castle Hill is today and was demolished in 1936.

Above: The Wheatsheaf, which was at No. 109 Castle Street, is shown here under snow in 1920. The Star Brewery, which supplied their beer, was originally situated on the site that is occupied by Rose Crescent today. The pub closed around 1970.

Left: The modern Rose pub, Rose Crescent in the 1960s; it eventually closed in 1981. It was built on the site of the old Rose tavern and its courtyard, which had been sold in 1817 to pay off the landlord's debts. The Rose is mentioned by Pepys in his diary: 'I, with my boy, Tom, whom I take with me, took coach … and came to Cambridge … and there at the Rose I met my father's horses … after supper to bed and there lay very ill by reason of some drunken scholars making a noise all night.' Twenty-four-hour drinking is not, after all, a twenty-first century phenomenon! The tavern housed a coffee house in 1815, serving tea and coffee and providing newspapers for their clientele. The old inn was demolished in 1821, after which Rose Crescent was developed by Charles Claydon and the new Rose built in 1826.

The Pickerel Inn in Magdalene Street, seen here decorated for the Coronation of Queen Elizabeth II in 1953, was built during the reign of the first Queen Elizabeth, although its frontage was rebuilt in the nineteenth century. The inn was frequented by boatmen and by porters from the nearby quayside, who used to watch cockfighting while waiting for boats to come in for unloading on the nearby Cam. A pickerel is a young pike.

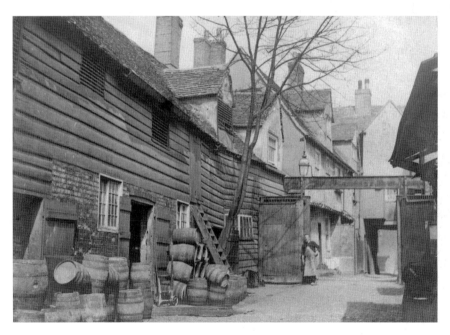

There were stables at the rear of the Pickerel Inn, as seen in this picture of Pickerel Yard, off Magdalene Street, around 1900. This was originally Bin Brook Lane, leading to a bridge over Bin Brook. In medieval times, the field leading to Bin Brook was covered in fishponds that belonged to St John's Hospital.

Left: The Cross Keys in Magdalene Street went out of business in the eighteenth century and became Cross Keys Yard, the site of student accommodation today. The inn was possibly frequented by such students as Samuel Pepys and Charles Kingsley, who were students at nearby Magdalene College.

Below: The True Blue, *c.* 1920. This inn, formerly the Lord Nelson, was situated on Sidney Street. After its closure in 1919, the area became the site of the Dorothy ballroom, café and restaurant.

Opposite above: The Dorothy was the venue for a dinner held in 1967 for the Saffron Walden Building Society and the firm of F.L. Unwin. The Dot, as it was affectionately called, was for many years the social centre of Cambridge, playing host to wartime dances and romances, afternoon tea dances, weddings, dinners and parties. In the 1970s it had four floors, each with a different style of music, from ballroom to disco, to cater for all tastes. Despite refurbishment, the Dot closed for good in 1989; the building now houses Waterstone's bookshop and the Life nightclub.

Below: The Eagle Inn, Benet Street is one ancient Cambridge inn that has survived and is flourishing today. It is on every tourist's list due to its wealth of history and its unique signed ceiling in the Air Force Bar. There are signatures of both British and American airmen, some of whom did not survive their bombing sorties from local airfields during the Second World War. There has been a tavern on the site for centuries, the site being acquired by Corpus Christi in 1488. Named the Eagle and Child in the past, it was a popular coaching inn; the galleried coaching yard still exists. Frequented by thousands of famous – and possibly infamous – past undergraduates, it has also achieved fame as the venue where Crick and Watson announced their discovery of DNA (helped by the unsung Rosalind Franklin, whose ideas they expanded). Pictured here in the 1930s, the exterior has changed little today.

The Little Rose was possibly a sixteenth-century inn; it was, until its demise in 1988, one of the oldest surviving Cambridge inns. It is now an oyster bar. The carrier and philanthropist Thomas Hobson, of 'Hobson's choice' fame (when you had no choice but to take the horse nearest the entrance, and so had no choice at all), is said to have stabled his horses there. It was a collection point for parcels until between the wars and was popular with American servicemen and RAF men and women during the Second World War. Undergraduates, college workers and Addenbrooke's staff all frequented its bars and in 1972 it had a bar called Ludwig's after the philosopher Wittgenstein, who had been a past customer. This photograph shows the stable entrance in 1938.

The Bull Hotel, Trumpington Street was also used by American servicemen, who affectionately called it Bull College, as they were able to have a term's study there while waiting to return home to America. These American personnel are standing outside the hotel around 1944. As the Bull stood between King's College and St Catharine's, or St Catz, it was said to have been built to stop cats looking at kings! It was formerly the Black Bull, which dated from Edward IV's reign; the later Bull was built in 1828 and in 1893 advertised itself as 'patronised by the Royal Family, Nobility and the Gentry'. After the Americans had left, the hotel became a student hostel.

The Golden Rose, *c.* 1912. Built in 1849, this tiny pub closed in 1971 and is now occupied by a firm of auctioneers. However, the Golden Rose emblem still blooms on the corner of the building in Emmanuel Road.

The Champion Of The Thames is the oldest pub in King Street, which was once home to up to fourteen pubs, and was named after an unknown rowing coach who became the licensee. It was part of the notorious King Street Run, once an initiative test for every fresher, in which they had to consume a pint of beer at each of up to ten pubs without 'peeing' or 'puking'. Other pubs were the King Street Run, the Bun Shop, the St Radegund, the Cambridge Arms, the Horse and Groom and the Duke of Cambridge. A newspaper account of November 1997 records that the time set for eight pints in eight pubs was 14 minutes 50 seconds. A similar event seems to be enacted in the centre of Cambridge on most weekends today.

The House of Commons at No. 66 Hills Road appears in trade directories between 1874 and 1969. In this 1962 picture, circus elephants are passing by. Dolphin's shoe repair shop was next door. Was this the first time dolphins and elephants had been seen at the House of Commons?

The Foresters, on the corner of Burleigh Street, survived until after the Grafton development, as can be seen in this 1984 photograph, but has now closed. At one time it was popular with townspeople and traders who frequented the nearby fairs.

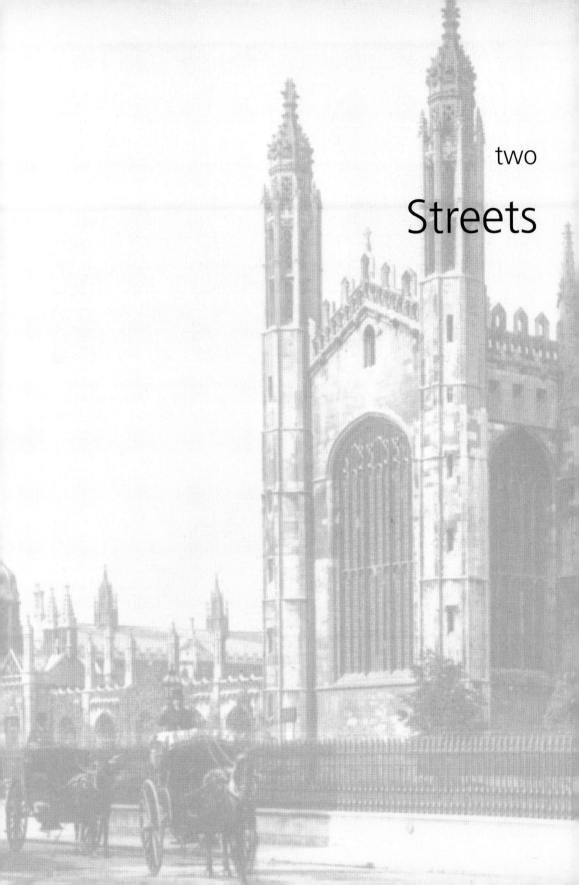

two

Streets

Petty Cury, looking east, *c*. 1909. The distinctive bay window of the Red Lion can be seen on the right. Petty Cury, situated in the very centre of Cambridge commerce, has for centuries been a very busy thoroughfare. The unusual name of the street is thought to have been derived from the Latin *Parva Cockeria* or Little Cury or Cooks' Row; Petty or Petit (Little) to distinguish it from the main cooks' row in Market Hill. It is believed to have contained many pastry cooks' booths and stalls and was for around 800 years lined with Cambridge's main inns. The Red Lion (after which the Lion Yard is named), the Falcon, the Red Hart, the Antelope and the Wrestlers Inn were all in this area and visiting royalty such as Elizabeth I and James I kept horses in the stables which lined the inn yards. Petty Cury was the first street to be cobbled in 1788. The area was redesigned by the Victorians in the late 1800s and in the 1970s was subject to major development.

Market Place, 1906. The medieval marketplace was, unlike the present one, L-shaped and Market Street was called Shoemaker Row or Cordwainer Street (cordwain was a special Spanish leather used for good-quality shoes). The marketplace was divided into distinct areas, with corn to the north and poultry, butter and meat to the south (Guildhall Street and Wheeler Street). The garden market was between the conduit and the Cross; the milk market was between the Cross and St Mary's Passage. Butter came by the yard and was then cut to size for the customer. The area was the traditional home of riots and demonstrations, and flogging and bull-baiting have also been recorded in the area.

Rose Crescent, c. 1890s. This Regency curve of shops was created in the 1820s in the courtyard of what was the Rose Tavern, which was once frequented by Pepys. The balcony to the right of the market entrance was where election results used to be announced to the throng gathered below. Rose Crescent is now home to upmarket shops and bars.

Peas Hill, showing the shops of Shrive the basketmakers, who also made wicker armchairs for undergraduates, and Fletcher the butcher, 1910. Peas Hill was the old fish market of Cambridge and has always been the centre of commerce. It was the site of the old Three Tuns Inn, later the Central Hotel and now a bank, which was where Pepys 'drank pretty hard, with many healths to the King' in 1660. A labyrinth of subterranean tunnels is to be found running underneath Peas Hill, one stretching all the way to the Round church. These have been used as wine cellars and, during the Second World War, as air-raid shelters for 400 people. The street was the scene of the 'Battle of Peas Hill' in 1820. This was a spectacular confrontation between town and gown caused by the acquittal of Queen Caroline (wife of George IV) after the unsuccessful Bill of Pains and Penalties, which tried to prove her guilty of improper conduct, was thrown out. The gownsmen, on the side of the Crown, were victorious.

Above: St John's Street during a funeral procession, *c.* 1900. The medieval Hospital of St John the Evangelist was situated here; it later became St John's College, which has been home to many distinguished scholars such as William Wordsworth, William Wilberforce, Lord Palmerston and Sir John Cockcroft, who worked on the atom at the Cavendish Laboratory. The D-Day landings were planned at a conference in the Combination Rooms there.

Left: All Saints in Jewry church, jutting out into St John's Street, *c.* 1860s. The area of All Saints Passage was a Jewish ghetto in the twelfth century, when Jews paid for safe places to stay. The church, which was on the site of All Saints Gardens, was demolished in 1865 and rebuilt in Jesus Lane.

Trinity Street, *c*. 1910. This street of mainly sixteenth-century buildings became, in the nineteenth century, home to a number of businesses, including booksellers and men's outfitters. At the premises of Macmillan publishers around the corner at No. 1 Trinity Street, Tennyson gave a reading of 'Maud' and Thackeray lunched with Daniel and Alex Macmillan. At No. 10, on the left of this picture, is the coaching inn the Blue Boar, where the Union London stagecoach called.

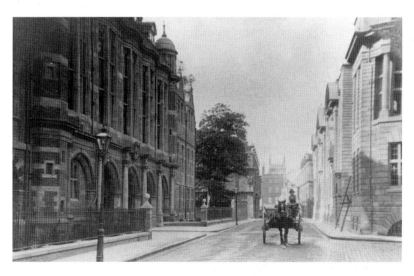

Downing Street, looking west from the junction with Corn Exchange Street, *c*. 1900. On the left is the Sedgwick Geology Museum. Downing Street has had many names, such as Dowdivers' Lane, Langreth or Langer Lane, Hogshill Lane and Bird Bolt Lane, after the hotel which stood on the junction with St Andrew's Street. Until the nineteenth century, the street was the site of many and various shops to cater for the university, with robemakers, wine importers, saddlers and even a dentist. All the shops were gradually replaced by university buildings and museums, and by 1939 all the buildings were owned by the university.

The Theatre of Anatomy, Queens Lane, 1815. The Anatomy Museum was built nearby, on the site of the original Botanical Gardens at the corner of Downing Street and Corn Exchange Street (or Slaughterhouse Lane), which is now the New Museums Site. In this museum, to an invited audience, galvanic experiments (using electric currents) were performed on cadavers collected from the gallows at Castle Hill. Murderers were seen to have no rights to a decent burial and were transported by cart from Castle Hill to be experimented on here. The bodies would then be dissected in front of the assembled townspeople – and ladies were seen to swoon! In 1833 the school was stormed by townsmen who believed the rumour (which turned out to be false) that a body had been disinterred for dissecting. The undergraduates fought to protect the school and won the day.

Portugal Place, *c.* 1930. The street was named after a cache of Portuguese coins found buried when the Georgian houses were built in the early nineteenth century. The houses were home to boatmen, ostlers and college servants but later became desirable residences. Francis Crick, of DNA fame, lived there in the 1950s; his house is today marked with a Golden Helix.

Round Church Street, before it was cleared to make access to the Park Street car park, which was built in 1961. The unusually shaped building in the centre was the barber's shop founded by Count Prziborsky, who had been barber to the Imperial Austrian Court.

Castle Street has had the reputation of being the street of many pubs, of hangings and of the Black Death in 1390. The remains of the castle stood here until 1842; the final building left standing was used as a prison until 1802. A new gaol was built in 1802, which stood until 1931. The slum clearances of the 1920s cleared away many of the old buildings and pubs and the court building on the right of the picture was demolished and lost its imposing statues in 1953.

Left: Kettle's Yard, *c.* 1900. Jim Ede took over a row of derelict houses here in 1956 and, over a period of sixteen years, renovated and extended them to house an eclectic range of artwork. Many of the exhibits were gifts from friends and artists he knew from the time when he was curator of the Tate Gallery in London. He moved to Edinburgh in 1973 and left the property to Cambridge University.

Below: Chesterton Road is a street of imposing town houses, built in the 1880s, many of which are now used as flats and for student lettings. They overlook the river and Jesus Lock and Green. The street was the home of the stables of the Cambridge Omnibus Co., which closed in 1902, and the site of the famous Cambridge Instrument Co.

Opposite above: Carlyle Road, looking from Chesterton Road to St Luke's church in the distance, *c.* 1910. There are more impressive late Victorian houses in this street.

Below: The opening of Victoria Avenue Bridge, 11 December 1890. The bridge was opened by Frederick Mace MA, Mayor of Cambridge and John Bester, chairman of the Chesterton Local Board. Originally known as Backside Road, Victoria Avenue ran through open fields, as shown in the Enclosure map of 1840. It is hard to imagine that this busy street, which ends in the gyratory at Mitcham's Corner, was once open countryside. Progress was helped by the construction of the bridge, which connected the street to the New Chesterton area that was being developed at the time. The bridge also provided a much-needed additional crossing over the river to relieve the other bridges in Bridge Street and Silver Street. Designed by engineers John Webster and Frank Waters, it was a fine example of late Victorian ironwork, with panels containing the arms of Cambridge and Chesterton and gaily painted.

Above: Sidney Street, 1920s. The Dorothy Restaurant can be seen on the right and Joshua Taylor's outfitters on the left. Sidney Street was part of the Via Devana, the Roman road from Colchester to Chester, and was named after Sidney Sussex College, which was built in 1595 on land where a Franciscan friary had stood. Oliver Cromwell studied here in 1616 but left on the death of his father to become a country squire and MP. The street is now home to many small shops; in the 1880s it was the fashion centre of Cambridge, with tailors, outfitters and clothiers mixed with residential family dwellings and university lodgings.

Left: Regent Street on a rainy evening in the 1960s. The street was once called Kingsway or Friars and Preachers Street. After 1815, when the Prince Regent passed through Cambridge, it became Regent Street and many houses were built there. The University Arms Hotel was built in 1833 as a coaching inn with large stables and a coach yard on the north side of its Park Terrace frontage. It had gardens behind, with tennis courts and a fives court. The Regent House Hotel (formerly the Glengarry), which had a disastrous fire in January 2003 and reopened in 2004, was home to the early Newnham College from 1871-1876. On the left of this picture, the gates of Downing College can be seen in the lamplight.

King's Parade, looking north, 1890. This world-famous street used to be called High Street and, between the sixteenth and nineteenth centuries, contained many houses, which were arranged in front of King's College. The railings in front of the college were removed in 1927 to open up the view of the Senate House.

King's Parade, looking south, 1890. Hansom cabs wait for hire on the rank in front of King's College.

Left: Corn Exchange Street was not named after the present Corn Exchange, which is on the corner of Wheeler Street, but after an earlier building built in 1842, at the Downing Street junction. The street was originally called Slaughterhouse Lane. In the nineteenth century it had many workshops and tiny overcrowded cottages, which were all demolished in 1975 to make way for the Lion Yard car park. Nine listed buildings were destroyed in the area; only Fisher House (formerly the Black Swan pub) and the Red Cow pub survived.

Below: Until the 1960s, Bradwell's Yard stood in the centre of Cambridge and contained several houses like the one in this photograph from the 1930s. These were demolished from 1957 and, in 1962, Bradwell's Court was built, housing twenty new shops. This central area is now awaiting redevelopment.

A 1900 engraving of St Andrew's Street, which shows the passage from pleasure to redemption in this 'Curious Group of Buildings in Cambridge', from the Fountain Inn to the police station, then the gaol (or Spinning House) and finally the Baptist Chapel. A police station was later built on the site of the Spinning House, which was a house of correction built by Thomas Hobson in 1628 to provide work for the unemployed and to house rogues and vagabonds. Prostitutes were also rounded up and kept there, and records show that the women were regularly flogged at a shilling a head. The building was later divided into two, with the prostitutes being kept in one side and the police station occupying the other. The police station is now Mandela House but a Fountain Inn still stands in the area.

Burleigh Street, c. 1890. The street was named after the carrier and mayor James Burleigh and, in the Victorian era, was a street of artisans and small shopkeepers. On the site of what is now the Robert Sayle department store, the Co-operative store was built. The Co-operative Society grew from the Cambridge Provident Industrial Society, which was formed in 1868 by a group of shoemakers who began co-operative trading. The Co-op was important to many poor families, who used the dividend as a form of saving to help clothe their families. The Foresters pub, seen here, was popular with people from visiting fairs.

Fitzroy Street, 1903. This street was part of the Kite area, which was demolished when the Grafton Centre was built. Originally home to nine pubs, in 1862 a Working Men's Club and Institute was built in the street, as an alternative social centre to the public houses for the self-improvement of the working classes. The institute had a library and held lectures, classes and exhibitions, and played an important role in the education of the working classes in the area. The bandstand of the Laurie and McConnal store can be seen high up on the left.

Mill Road, c. 1906. Until the Enclosure Act of 1806, Mill Road was mainly open fields, except for the windmill (which stood opposite Emery Street) that gave the road its name. In 1838 the Union Workhouse was built in Mill Road, as far out of town as possible. It was used during the Second World War as a hospital for troops, then became a maternity home and is now called Ditchburn Place. With the coming of the railway in 1845, Mill Road expanded, providing houses for railway workers. However, the Romsey Town end remained undeveloped until around 1879. Mill Road Bridge was built in 1889, which brought further expansion.

three

Wheels

A horse and carriage waits outside E. Glasscock, cab proprietors, in Newnham Road, 1900. Because the station was built so far from the centre of Cambridge – some say because the university was afraid that undergraduates would abscond – cab proprietors like this one had a lucrative trade ferrying passengers to and fro from the centre.

Hansom cabs and cabmen waiting for fares in Station Road in the 1910s. Cabmen had to be careful how long they waited, as they could be fined for loitering for too long!

Cambridge station, *c*. 1900. The station was opened in 1845 and gradually revolutionised supply routes; traditionally, the rivers Cam and Ouse were the way that goods such as timber, grain, bricks and osiers reached Cambridge from King's Lynn and the Fens.

Cambridge station, *c*. 1920. Initially, the railway company was not able to run trains on a Sunday between 10 a.m. and 5 p.m. because of religious objections. Plans put forward for stations on Christ's Pieces, Silver Street and Queen Anne Terrace were vetoed by the university.

A horse-drawn double-decker tram in Station Road, c.1914. The Cambridge Street Tramways Co. was founded in 1880 and ran horse-drawn trams, both single- and double-decker, to and fro on single tracks. The trams ran from the station via Hills Road and Regent Street to Christ's College, with diversions from Hyde Park Corner along Lensfield Road and King's Parade to Market Hill, then to their depot in East Road via Gonville Place. Each car was pulled by a single horse and was quite slow; it was often joked that, if in a hurry, it was quicker to walk!

This photograph from February 1914 possibly shows the last horse-drawn tram, in East Road. Cambridge undergraduates, with instruments such as trombones and bugles, played dirges during the last trip and a riot almost ensued, with the police being called. Students ran amok, turning off gas lamps, breaking a shop window and attempting to set fire to a bandstand in Christ's Pieces. Electric trams were never introduced in Cambridge because it was thought that the overhead cables would be unsightly.

A Cambridge Omnibus Co. open-top horse-bus outside the Wheatsheaf pub in High Street, Chesterton. The company ran between 1896 and 1902, and charged a penny fare from the station to the city centre. They had too few customers and more than a few accidents!

Until the advent of motor 'horsepower', Cambridge ran horse-drawn corporation dustcarts. Fred Gawthrop is seen here with one of the carts, No. 46, in Union Lane.

CAMBRIDGE UP TO DATE!

Above: This is a 25hp Straker-Squire belonging to the Cambridge University & Town Motor Omnibus Co. on Market Hill, probably on its first day in 1905. This company was one of two companies running buses in Cambridge but there were many accidents, including one occasion when the conductor fell off the footplate and was run over and killed by his own bus. The buses also damaged kerbs and shop awnings and filled the streets with choking black exhaust smoke. In 1906 all operations ceased.

Left: This cartoon shows some of the concerns people had about the buses! Note the poor dog squashed under the wheels, the broken lamp-post and the terrified passengers – is the man on the left praying?

A double-decker open-top Scott-Stirling in De Freville Avenue, *c.* 1908. In 1907 James Berry Walford started the Ortona Bus Co., naming it after a cruise ship he had seen while in the Adriatic. The buses had green livery, red wheels and red-trimmed bodywork. The maximum speed allowed at the time was 12mph.

An Ortona motorbus taking the staff of Hallack and Bond, wholesale grocers, of Market Hill on a trip to Southend, *c.* 1924. The Ortona company was taken over by Eastern Counties in 1931.

Drummer Street bus station, looking east. There was parking for thirty-five private cars as well as buses. The large trees in the central island were once part of Christ's Pieces. There was a battle between the council and townspeople when the bus station was built in 1925, as it took part of the 'people's garden'. A mass protest involving around 3,000 people took place because the council had started work before approval had been granted. Protesters were carried in a cart, with the horse being replaced by supporters who pulled the 'tumbril' to the mayor's house to protest. The trees have since disappeared but the resistance to growth goes on, despite the bus station being hopelessly overcrowded.

The first electric brougham, or closed carriage, to arrive in Cambridge is seen here in 1890 outside The Hermitage in Silver Street, with Revd Stephen Parkinson, the Praelector of St John's College, inside. The house was built by corn and coal merchant Mr S. Beales, who owned a quay, a granary and a warehouse in Cambridge, and is now part of Darwin College. The first motor car recorded in Cambridge was a four-seater single-cylinder Peugeot, driven by C.S. Rolls, of Rolls Royce fame, in 1897.

John Chivers owned this motor car, seen outside the St Andrew's Street Baptist Chapel in around 1910. The car is being driven by chauffeur W.B. Smith.

Mayor George Stace and Chief Constable C.E. Holland leave Cambridge by car for the Coronation of King George V in 1911.

This sporty number was photographed in Queen's Road, with King's College in the background. Undergraduates could hire sports cars for a day's outing from one of the car-hire firms which sprang up during the motor boom years of the 1910s.

Mechanics at King and Harper's are seen here proudly posing with the racing car *Bluebird III* in 1900. The firm was established in 1900 during the cycle boom and went on to manufacture motorcycles and to repair cars. The firm had four depots in Cambridge and employed around 250 people at one time. Both partners won medals, including a gold medal at Crystal Palace in 1902 for their British motorcycle with a foreign engine. They were friends with Charles Rolls, of Rolls Royce fame.

This motor show held in the 1910s shows the popularity of both motor cars and motorcycles at the time. It also shows the interior of the Corn Exchange before its metamorphosis into a concert venue in the 1980s.

Other wheeled contraptions were also taking to the streets, like this bath chair being navigated around Portugal Place around 1910. Bath chairs were the forerunner of the modern motorized wheelchairs that zip around today.

Above: This bicycle-towed rickshaw was conceived, constructed and used by Harry Newell, a Cambridge cycle-shop proprietor, around 1900. However, it did not succeed. The idea was tried again in 1996 and 1999 but, although it seemed the answer to fast travel during congestion, there were problems with licensing so the idea did not get up and running.

Left: This early tricycle looks hard work but was obviously lots of fun. Note the fact that the men are wearing backwards-facing hats – not, after all, just a twenty-first-century fashion statement!

A traction engine pulls a large boat on a trailer along Huntingdon Road, 1910. Steam power meets horsepower; I wonder who gave way?

New Square, with cows gently grazing. This was before its conversion to a car park in the 1930s.

New Square car park in the 1950s. In 1983 the park was covered in grass again; only in Cambridge could a useful car park close to the shops be converted back to a grassy park! Less useful but more pleasing to the eye, this park is now a pleasant walk from the city centre to the Grafton Centre.

Traffic congestion at the junction of Emmanuel Street and St Andrew's Street in 1929, as Ortona bus CE 6011 attempts to turn the corner.

four

River

The River Cam provides a great source of pleasurable pursuits, such as punting, rowing and boating, in beautiful surroundings. Punting on the River Cam, as here at Grantchester in 1920, is one of the images of Cambridge life that is famous the world over due to the more than four million tourists and countless foreign students who visit Cambridge every year. Fen punts have been used since medieval times to carry crops, reedcutters, wildfowlers and fishermen around the Fens, but pleasure punting is thought to have come to Cambridge around 1903 when the long and elegant Thames punts arrived here. Early punt-hirers were Dolby, Strange, Mathie, Reynolds, Banham, Scudamore and Bullen. The trip two miles upstream to Grantchester Meadows is the most popular route, with afternoon cream teas at the Orchard tea rooms, where time just might stand still.

Bullen's boatyard, Fisher's Lane, 1960s. Punting is still very popular and Scudamore's now have one of the largest punting operations in Europe. In Cambridge the punter stands at the back of the punt; in Oxford they stand at the front. The Backs are world famous for their beauty, and the River Cam passes through some of the finest college gardens in the country. Trinity College Library, which was built by Wren, King's College Chapel and the bridges of Clare and Queens are some of the highlights seen along the way.

Fisher's Lane, looking towards Magdalene Bridge, *c.* 1910. Magdalene Bridge was earlier known as the Great Bridge and was the main bridge of Cambridge, where goods for the colleges were disembarked. The chimney in the distance belongs to the Thompson's Lane electric power station, owned by the Cambridge Electric Supply Co., established in 1892. The power station was one of the first to use steam turbines, for which quantities of water was needed, hence the position beside the river; it was built despite opposition from Magdalene College. At first, power was produced just for lighting and the current was switched on only after dark. Production ceased in 1966 when electricity came from substations at Burwell and Fulbourn, feeding off the National Grid. The chimney was demolished in 1982.

A Licensed Victuallers Association outing aboard the steamboat *Otter*, seen here passing through Jesus Green Lock, 1890. The *Otter* was just one of the many pleasure boats working on the Cam at the time. Banham's boat-hire company ran daily excursions to Clayhithe and weekly trips to Ely. Private parties also were held aboard the passenger boats.

The steamboat *Butterfly* on the Cam, 1907. The owner, J.A.F. Fuller, and his son, who is holding the baby, are on board.

Visiting royalty also enjoyed a river trip while in Cambridge. In July 1963 Princess Margaret and Lord Snowden took a trip on the *Marchioness of Bury* after visiting Banham's boatyard and W.G. Pye's factory.

The first steamboat race, between *Kathleen*, owned by a Mr Leach, and *Sunbeam*, owned by a Mr Barlow, took place in 1936 on the Cam. *Kathleen* won the day.

The steam launch *Artemis*, the last of her type on the Cam, 1960. She was originally built for a millionaire in 1899 as a tender to his seagoing yacht and was restored by A.F. Leach.

The beautiful setting of the Cam is ideal for the spectators watching the races, but for rowers there are a few problems. This scene in the 1900s shows spectators at the May 'bumps' races. The traditional sport of 'bumping' is thought to have developed due to the narrowness of the Cam, which made it difficult to run races with boats side by side. In 1825, when both Trinity and St John's Colleges got an eight-oared boat, they began to bump. One would row upriver and sound a bugle, then the second boat would follow and try to catch and bump the first boat; if successful, the boats would change places. The winning boat would be Head of the River.

The May bumps, 1920. Christ's College's first boat is bumping Jesus College's second boat.

The May races at Ditton Corner on Wednesday 8 June 1910. Marquees would be set up in the Paddock, strawberry and cream teas would be served and swingboats and roundabouts would be set up in Chesterton Fields. Both races and balls in Cambridge were originally held in May but had to be delayed until June due to pressure of examinations; they are, however, still described as being in May!

The Cambridge University crew for the 1886 Boat Race. The Boat Race between Oxford and Cambridge Universities has taken place since 1829, when the course was at Henley-on-Thames (Oxford won after a restart). The Putney to Mortlake course has been used since 1849, except for a break during the Second World War. In 1944 the race was held on the river Ouse at Queen Adelaide, Ely; there was a commemorative race in 2004 on the same stretch of river. Other wartime venues were Henley and Sandford.

Above: Skaters on the Cam, 1929. They are skating on the stretch of river opposite Trinity College Library.

Left: Skaters had another rare opportunity to skate on the Cam in January 1963. Air frost was recorded on twenty-eight nights during the month of January; the lowest temperature recorded was -40°F on the ground at Oakington. A Mini was seen parked on the river at Ely and boats froze into the harbour at Wisbech docks, like a scene from the Baltic.

Opposite above: The river was not only a playground, it was also a place of work. The steam tug *Olga* and tank barges *Lizzie* and *Enid* are seen here taking on gas water at Cambridge gasworks around 1910. Gas water was the by-product of town gas and was a filthy black liquid very rich in ammonia, therefore it was valuable in the manufacture of artificial fertilisers and manures. The gas water was transported to factories in King's Lynn by barge until 1938, when road tankers took over.

Below: The Cam from Stourbridge Common, 1960s. This view combines beauty with utility, with the gasworks in the distance. John Grafton brought gas to Cambridge in the early nineteenth century. Although it was not the first location, eventually this gasworks was built close to the river so that the coal, which was used in gas manufacture, could easily be unloaded. The Cambridge Gaslight Co. was set up in 1826, bringing light to the murky streets of Cambridge. The gasworks were demolished in 2001 to be replaced by a supermarket.

Above: Quayside, looking east, 1930s. A river scene with the electricity works in the background. The company needed large quantities of water for condensing.

Left: An atmospheric river scene, 1960s. The electricity works provide a backdrop.

Opposite above: The Ferry Path or Fort St George ferry, looking from the Fort St George pub to Ferry Path, *c.* 1930. Before bridges were built over the Cam, ferries would convey people across the river at several strategic points. The Fort St George public house was on an island until Jesus Lock was constructed. The ferry was a direct link to Chesterton before Victoria Bridge was built.

Below: Originally ferries would be poled across the river but by the nineteenth century a chain and wheel was installed on the boats and the ferryman would 'grind' the passengers across the river. The Red Grind at the Plough Fen Ditton, pictured in 1905, was popular during the May races. However, this ferry had a history of tragic accidents, like the one in June 1905 when three women were drowned, weighed down by their voluminous skirts, which tangled in the chain under the boat. The accident was caused by exuberant undergraduates who jumped onto the ferry at the last moment, causing it to lurch, which snapped the chain and overturned the boat. Ferries began to die out in the 1920s and 1930s, when more bridges were built across the Cam, thus ending a way of life for the ferry families.

Above: A Banham's craft, the *Duchess*, was converted for firefighting during the Second World War.

Left: Punting on the Cam, 1947. Once the bombs stopped falling and student life returned to normal, the river again became the scene of gentle tranquillity.

five

War

Army Airship Beta II, in Jesus Grove. Cambridge. Sep. 16th 1912

The airship *Beta II* was involved in aerial operations during the large-scale military manoeuvres that took place in Cambridge in September 1912. This was a huge undertaking, with thousands of troops and horses and several planes converging on the area as part of a major military operation in East Anglia. Soldiers, including the 3rd and 4th Divisions and several brigades of Territorials, arrived in Cambridge and the surrounding villages. An aeroplane camp was set up at Hardwick; two pilots were involved in a fatal disaster when their monoplane crashed near Hitchin. The object of the whole exercise was to learn lessons and gain experience of a battle situation. This was the first ever practice of aerial reconnaissance, which would prove invaluable during the First World War. The King visited the area, staying at Trinity College and surveying the troops on the Gog Magog hills, seated on a charger. The operations were directed by General Sir John French and also involved was General Sir Douglas Haig, both of whom would be heard of later.

Soldiers were again seen in Cambridge at the start of the First World War. In September 1914, the Army's 6th Division were camped on Jesus Green, and also on the Commons. Local residents looked after the soldiers, bringing them pails of water, hot meals and fruit.

Officers in training at Emmanuel College during the First World War. Cambridge had a very different atmosphere to normal at this time because there were no students. Troops took their places in the local lodging houses and officers were trained in the colleges. Some 150 boy refugees from Belgium arrived in June 1916; they were housed initially in the Lion Hotel, then in private houses. Eventually, there was a widespread shortage of food, with butchers having to close at some point due to a lack of available meat and high prices. The blackout was introduced in May 1915 amid fears of enemy attack, fears which were reinforced when a Zeppelin crossed over the town in September 1915.

Military bicycles in Market Square during troop mobilisations, 1914. The Gothic fountain in the centre of the square was built in 1855 and taken down in 1953, when it became unsafe.

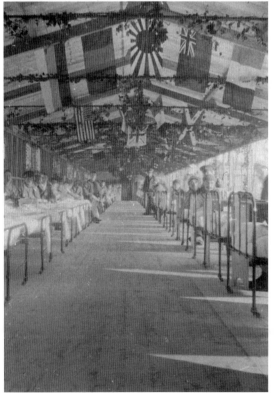

Above: The First Great Eastern Hospital, with tents on the lawns of Trinity College, at the beginning of the First World War. The hospital served wounded soldiers; sick and wounded servicemen were treated both in tents and in the actual college buildings.

Left: The hospital later moved into huts on the site of the present University Library in West Road. This picture of one of the huts shows that they had open sides. Fresh air was thought to do the patients good at the time, hence the hats and coats being worn!

Lord French inspecting a parade of volunteer training corps and Serbian boy refugees on Market Hill in 1916.

A hungry-looking crowd queuing for potatoes outside S. Green & Sons in Mill Road, April 1917. Civilians suffered shortages during the First World War and women were trained in farm labouring at Girton in order to increase the production of fresh fruit and vegetables for the local population.

Military horses cooling down in the Cam. This practice was not without its dangers and at least one soldier had to be rescued from drowning.

Victory at last! The war had dragged on long past the predicted Christmas 1914, with many thousands of young men killed, including Grantchester poet Rupert Brooke, whose poignant war poems are still read and remembered. This triumphal burning of an effigy of the Kaiser, held on a bayonet, took place at the end of the war in 1918, on Market Hill. Celebrations became a little out of hand and there were newspaper reports of widespread hooliganism taking place.

Victory parade, 1919. The parade was delayed until the final peace treaty was signed in 1919. Demobbed servicemen in civilian clothes pass along Petty Cury into St Andrew's Street.

With the onset of the Second World War in 1939, precautionary measures had to be taken and these bewildered children are being issued with gas masks in Ramsden Square. During the Second World War, evidence of war was all around in Cambridge: there were trenches in Midsummer Common, shelters on Parker's Piece and sandbags on all major buildings. Railings were torn up to be melted down for the war effort and the glass was even removed from the windows of King's College Chapel in case of damage by enemy bombing. Blackouts were enforced and petrol was rationed.

Bomb damage in Vicarage Terrace, June 1940. Despite the precautions, there were casualties of war.
Ten people died when this bomb dropped and others died too in Cherry Hinton Road, Great Eastern
Street and in the Bridge Street area. The true story about what went on was only revealed after the
war, due to the strict censorship in operation during it. No mention could be made about the weather,
the Royal Family or any bombing or air-crash locations; the press would only report those as having
happened 'somewhere in East Anglia'. This secrecy was necessary to prevent the enemy from getting vital
information which could help them in their efforts against us.

Opposite above: This sandbagged building, next to the old Cambridge post office in Petty Cury, was a
gas-mask distribution centre. It later became a British Restaurant and was known as the Civic
Restaurant.

Opposite below: Cambridge police station, St Andrew's Street was protected by an impressive array of
sandbags in 1939. The police station is now Mandela House.

Cambridge played generous host to thousands of evacuees from bomb-stricken London and other major cities, as the threat from Hitler's Luftwaffe loomed. These were mainly children but some mothers and sick and wounded civilians eventually arrived too. In September 1939 around 3,000 children arrived in Cambridge from London, Manchester, Birmingham, Glasgow, Liverpool and Leeds, as a precautionary measure before the war started. Each child carried a gas mask, some food, a change of clothes and three labels, which they were given instructions not to chew! They were reported to have behaved impeccably on their arrival, with only a few tears.

Evacuee children visiting Cambridge market in 1944. Not all the children were as happy as these little mites seem, with some complaints that Cambridge was a dull and dismal place, with little entertainment and a lack of youth centres and facilities for children. The lack of a decent bus service and of new films in the local cinemas were also frequent complaints. Some did not like their foster parents, finding them too 'posh' compared to their Cockney parents, and some complained that their foster mothers could not cook. Many evacuees missed their families and returned to the cities again, despite the threat of bombing raids. Visits by worried parents were organised at the weekends on buses and some fathers cycled from the East End to visit their families. Two small children were also found hitchhiking back to London on their own.

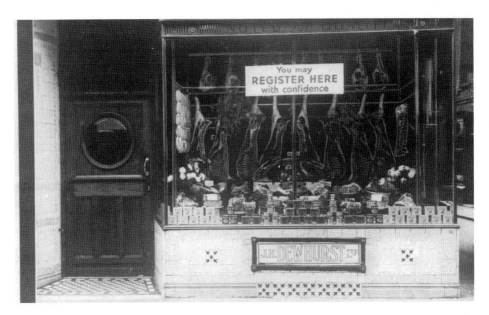

Dewhurst's butchers in Petty Cury, displaying a sign urging people to register for rationed meat inside. Rationing of food and petrol had to be introduced, as they became more difficult to obtain as the war dragged on. Potatoes were grown in the grounds of St John's College and the Women's Land Army, who were mainly girls from London, were trained at the university farm in the production of vital food for the civilian population.

A.E. Whitehead's fruiterers at No. 306 St Andrew's Street urged people to 'help to win the war' by recycling paper bags and wrappers. We are only now getting back into the recycling habits that were practised during the war.

Lorries like these ran on gas during the war to conserve petrol, which was an idea later adopted in Cambridge city centre with the environmentally friendly green Shuttlebus.

Air cadets drilling on Parkside, complete with gas masks.

Members of the armed forces celebrate at Cambridge YMCA, Christmas 1942. The war was not all gloom and doom, a good time could be had as well. Vera Lynn and Wilfred Pickles came to Cambridge as part of ENSA (Entertainments National Service Association) and there were regular dances at the Dorothy, where the presence of American GIs and the dashing pilots who were being trained at Marshall's aerodrome caused a stir.

When victory came at last, Cambridge erupted with delight and many streets held street parties with any food they had managed to save for the event. This Victory tea party was held in Hobart Road in 1945.

This happy crowd is pictured on VE Day at the Romsey Ward children's tea party. One story is that, in order to give children jelly, tin baths were filled with orange squash and gelatine; one wonders if there was a flavour of carbolic in the recipe!

VE celebrations in Market Hill, 1945. When the news of the peace came, crowds gathered, there was dancing and singing in the streets to the music of marching bands, and bonfires and home-made fireworks were lit.

six

Women

Laundry workers at Trumpington, 1900. Women played an important role in the Cambridge service industry in the nineteenth century; with the needs of a large population of male undergraduates to cater for, the university has always needed laundry workers. Clothes would be washed by hand and either dried on Laundress Green or on lines like cobwebs across yards and streets.

Left: A 'bedder' was a woman employed to do domestic chores in the residential rooms of the colleges. In the days of coal fires, distant bathrooms and no piped water, they were a necessity. However, female students at Girton College were expected to clean their own rooms and perform domestic tasks, as well as studying.

Opposite above: The surgical ward of Addenbrooke's Hospital, 1888. Nursing was one of the few areas of employment for women in late Victorian times. Addenbrooke's actively sought 'a better sort of nurse' in the 1860s, taking measures to make nursing an acceptable career. The original Addenbrooke's Hospital was built in 1766 with money from the estate of John Addenbrooke, who died in 1719 leaving a bequest to provide for a hospital for the poor. It was rebuilt in 1864 on the same site in Trumpington Street, on the opposite side of the road to the Fitzwilliam Museum. The old Addenbrooke's Hospital is now the Judge Institute. The hospital moved to Hills Road in the 1960s; it was opened by the Queen in 1962.

Below: The Cambridge Temperance Jubilee and Band of Hope Procession in 1907. The Temperance Movement was one area that women became involved in, and the first Women's Temperance Society was formed in Cambridge in 1869. Members were concerned about the effects of alcohol on the poor families of Cambridge and they campaigned for a reduction in the number of public houses and for an improvement in standards. A survey in 1906 found several hundred pubs in Cambridge, which caused the Temperance Movement great consternation. The Band of Hope, a branch of the Temperance Movement, was started in Brewery Yard, Magdalene Street in 1861. Temperance literature used homilies like this:

Destroyer of the constitution   **K**indler of strife
Robber of the pocket   **A**ssassinator of the human race
Unerring pathway to the grave   **R**eproach of character
Never failing producer of misery   **D**estroyer of the soul

A National Union of Women's Suffrage Society stall on Peas Hill, with ladies canvassing support for women's franchise. Cambridge had a thriving suffrage movement, with three leagues: the Cambridge Women's Suffrage Association, the Church League for Women's Suffrage and even a Cambridge University Men's League for Women's Suffrage. Prominent local supporters were Emily Davies, who started Girton College, Dame Millicent Fawcett and Mrs Rackham, a relative of Arthur Rackham, the famous illustrator. Emmeline and Sylvia Pankhurst both visited Cambridge to speak at the Guildhall on several occasions, usually to an antisocial crowd containing heckling undergraduates. The undergraduates would ring bells, let off stinkbombs and blow whistles and trumpets to disrupt the speeches but they were met with calm and dignified ladies who heartily believed in their cause. The speakers justified the use of violent means as, in the past, women had been treated with 'legal, political and social injustice in being denied the vote'. There were some acts of militancy in Cambridge, such as when a house in Storey's Way was set on fire by Norwich schoolteacher Miriam Pratt, who was released from Holloway prison after five days' hunger strike. Church services were disrupted, and the new gates of St John's College were daubed with the suffragette colours of purple, green and white and the slogan 'Votes for Women' written on the paintwork.

A Cambridge Women's Suffrage Association procession in St John's Street, July 1913. This was part of a national suffrage pilgrimage that converged on Hyde Park, London from all over the country. A group of local ladies joined the march to London via Royston, accompanied part of the way by the Sawston band. The pilgrims covered an average of eight to ten miles daily. However, it was not the militant suffragette action that secured the vote but the way that women ably coped with men's jobs during the First World War, which secured the respect of their menfolk and resulted in them gaining the vote in 1918.

The Dr Barnardo's Bazaar in 1910 attracted many women who had become actively involved in charity work, particularly in the area of social welfare. Dr Barnardo had visited Cambridge in 1896 and spoke of his work helping orphaned children, some of whom, he said, had come from Cambridge.

Women became clerks, postwomen, van drivers, conductresses, window cleaners and street cleaners. This picture shows women street cleaners with Cambridge Corporation dustcart No. 1, 1917.

Left: Female employees of the Cambridge post office in 1919, including a sorter, a postwoman and a telegraph messenger.

Below: The Cambridge telephone exchange, with women at the switchboard, *c.* 1914. The telephone exchange was in Post Office Terrace. Local calls were unlimited but trunk calls were timed and the telephonist would interrupt after three minutes and ask, 'Your three minutes are up, do you wish to go on?'.

Above: Women workers shovelling coke at the gasworks, *c.* 1918.

Right: Two female window cleaners working for the Cambridge Window Cleaning Co. in Hobson Street, 1916.

Women conductors working for the Ortona Bus Co. in 1919.

One way in which women demonstrated their independence was by riding bicycles or, in this case, tricycles. The more racy women wore bloomers or divided skirts, *c.* 1890.

The Girton College fire brigade, 1887. Emily Davies, who campaigned for the vote for women, was one of the first to realise that nothing would change for women until they received equal opportunities in education, particularly higher education. She founded Girton College in 1869, at a time when higher education was thought by many to be bad for women's health; it was believed that the sheer exertion of study would push women into mental or physical illness. Educated women, it was thought, would be unsuitable marriage partners, who would be unable to carry out domestic or social duties. Girton girls, therefore, had much to prove and had to endure primitive and austere conditions at Girton and not a little prejudice from the wider university. However, they were often quite formidable, even running their own college fire brigade.

Although female students quickly found success in examinations, they were not allowed to officially receive degrees. In May 1897 a university poll was held to debate the issue. Crowds, estimated at 15,000–20,000 people, gathered outside the Senate House and the situation turned into a near-riot. An effigy of a woman in bloomers was suspended above Macmillan and Bowes' booksellers. Undergraduates lit a bonfire on Market Square and did hundreds of pounds worth of damage, throwing lighted fireworks and smashing windows. Between twenty and thirty panes of glass were broken by flying missiles such as oranges, eggs and rockets. The vote went against granting degrees to women by 1,713 votes to 662. Similar polls in 1920 and 1921 again met with defeat, and it was 1948 before women were fully granted degrees on the same basis as men.

A close-up of the figure in bloomers
suspended above the crowds during
the university poll in 1897.

This theatrical group presents a spoof on the equality question, with a staged photograph in 1900.
The situation pictured would have, at the time, only been wishful thinking for women at Girton and
Newnham, for fraternising with male undergraduates was not encouraged.

The late Queen Mother (then Queen Elizabeth) was the first to receive an honorary degree in 1948. Several past lady graduates received their degrees in a special ceremony at the same time. The Queen visited Girton and Newnham Colleges after the ceremony, where the students took off their gowns and waved them in the air. The gowns were symbols of the students' newly granted right to full university membership.

Girton girls won a reputation for being formidable. They were expected to act with propriety and initially were chaperoned everywhere so that not a whiff of scandal damaged the reputation of the college. They were also encouraged to play sports such as tennis to keep fit and were seen to be healthier than their Newnham counterparts. In the early days, players were expected to play in an impeccably feminine style, with no vigorous stretching or running and while wearing long skirts.

W.E. Gladstone planting a tree in Newnham College grounds, 1887. The tree was later dug up and removed by Tory undergraduates. Newnham College was founded by Henry Sidgwick in 1871. He disagreed with Emily Davies and set up his own small college with five female students at No. 74 Regent Street, which later became the Glengarry Hotel. In the 1970s women began to be admitted to the men's colleges and women now make up more than half of the university intake (53 per cent in 2003). There is currently a female Vice Chancellor, Professor Alison Richard.

Homerton College students in the library, 1940s. The college was originally founded in London; it moved to the Cambridge site in 1894 and was housed in the empty buildings of Cavendish College. It became well known for the training of teachers and, in the early 1900s, became a women-only college. Female teachers were expected to be single and they had to give up work if they married.

Women preparing food for a cadet camp, 1944. Once again, wartime proved to be the time when women's true worth was seen, whether it was in support of the forces or in skilled factory and office work, and many women academics pitched in with menial tasks when necessary.

The Women's Voluntary Service collecting food scraps from the market to be fed to pigs. The WVS also undertook the making of camouflage nets. The service later became known as the Women's Royal Voluntary Service.

Servicemen and women relaxing together at the Toc H lounge in Corn Exchange Street, 1943.

seven

Shops

Above: A.B. Cornell's shop at No. 296 Mill Road, *c.* 1900. The shop sold game, which can be seen hanging outside, and fruit and fish, which were arranged inside. Game was a cheap source of meat at a time when chicken was not widely available and mutton was often too tough to eat. It was an alternative to pork, which was the staple diet of every country family.

Left: Petty Cury, looking east from Market Square, decorated for the Coronation of George V in 1911. George Morley's wine and spirit merchants, at No. 1a, and A.R. Nichols' butchers can be seen. Cambridge always loved a celebration, getting out the bunting at every available opportunity.

Above: Although many popular shops have disappeared from Cambridge in the past few years, one popular Cambridge name that still exists today is Heffer's. The bookshop and stationer's business began in 1876 in Fitzroy Street. The firm moved into the city centre to Petty Cury in 1896 and to Sidney Street, where for some years they also had a stationery department.

Right: Abbey Stores, No. 131 Newmarket Road, with Mrs Haynes at the counter, *c.* 1910. In these days of supermarkets and hypermarkets, some older people remember with nostalgia shops like these, with their myriad smells of coffee beans, bacon and spices and the tubs of dried goods like tea, flour and sugar, whose contents would be weighed to order and emptied into paper bags, instead of sealed in the ubiquitous plastic of today.

William Bell's butchers, No. 59 Ross Street, with the staff posing outside, *c.* 1910. William Bell is the man wearing the apron; he is accompanied by his sister and delivery boy Gilbert Barber. Mr Bell kept the shop for around fifty years and it was one of the first shops in Cambridge to boast a refrigerator, which everyone came to see.

George Moon's drapers, No. 107 Fitzroy Street, 1915. It is said that at the turn of the twentieth century, women would redeem their husbands' suits from Morley's or Bradley's pawnbrokers in the street nearby, then buy a halfpenny collar and a halfpenny dickey (a false shirt front) from Moon's, so that they could go to church on Sunday looking their best.

International Stores, another Fitzroy Street shop, with its smart shop assistants posing proudly outside. An army of delivery boys would carry customers' orders to their homes, with groceries precariously perched on their trade bicycles.

Yet another shop that has long since disappeared is that of F. Suttle, tailor, at No. 133 Fitzroy Street. This whole area changed forever in the 1980s, when the Kite area – so-called because of the shape of planned development area – became home to the Grafton Centre.

The popular Laurie and McConnal department store, seen here in the 1960s, was another casualty of the Kite plans. The store opened in 1883 and was rebuilt in 1903 after a disastrous fire. It was forced to close in 1977, due to indecision about the projected plans for the Grafton Centre, with the loss of 100 jobs. The distinctive bandstand was added in 1903. It was used regularly at first and the Cambridge Town Band would play to entertain Saturday afternoon shoppers, while cream teas and ice cream was served on the roof garden. In 1975 eight members of a local jazz group squeezed into the bandstand to protest about the possible closure, but to no avail.

Another family department store which has disappeared is that of W. Eaden Lilley & Co. Ltd of Market Street, seen here in 1900. The Eaden Lilley partnership was born from scandal, when one of William Eaden's daughters eloped with David Lilley, son of a Bourn farmer. Reconciliation took place and the couple's son, who was born William Eaden Lilley in 1816, soon became the sole owner of the company, which developed into a department store after 1890. The store closed in 1999 after 250 years of business, leaving 125 employees out of work, to make way for the present Borders bookshop.

Right: A portrait of W. Eaden Lilley, *c.* 1900. This image is from a collection of over 40,000 glass negatives from the famous Palmer Clarke photographers, which Cambridge Central library is in the process of digitising.

Below: An interior shot of Eaden Lilley's in 1920, redolent with the smell of Sunlight and carbolic soap. There are many recognisable objects and brand names on the shelves.

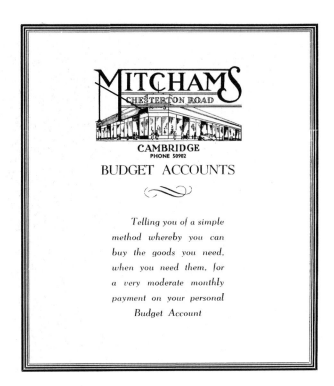

Left: A billhead for Mitcham's in Chesterton Road.

Mitcham's drapery store on the corner of Chesterton Road and Victoria Avenue was established in 1909. Charles Mitcham continued on the site until 1944, when the business was sold to a London firm called Dupont Bros, who astutely kept the name Mitcham's until 1977. The corner soon became known as Mitcham's Corner, a name that still endures today to describe the busy gyratory system.

Above: Stockbridge's was another old family firm; it was run by W. Stockbridge, seen here on the right outside his Sidney Street furniture shop, acquired in 1881, which is now the Alliance and Leicester Building Society. The dogs' drinking bowls placed strategically beside the legs of the tables on show were to stop passing dogs using the legs for other purposes. The firm were originally furniture dealers and upholsterers, supplying furniture to undergraduates who, each year, would arrive to an empty room, so there was a lucrative market in furniture. The firm also undertook interior decoration and sold small antiques and jewellery. During the Second World War, no one wanted to invest in antiques and expensive furniture which could be bombed the next day, so the firm concentrated on selling rings and jewellery to American GIs as presents for their girlfriends. After the war, when the market improved, Stockbridge's again specialised in antiques and, eventually, had another store in Bridge Street.

Right: Walter Stockbridge, founder of the firm, 1845-1923.

Left: Joshua Taylor's Sidney Street store, decorated for Christmas in the 1960s. Joshua Taylor I opened his first shop in Ely in 1810 and his son, Joshua Taylor II, then opened the Sidney Street store, soon expanding to Nos 58 and 60. The store opened in 1860 in a blaze of gaslight and provided top-quality clothing. To begin with, it was staffed entirely by men; women were not allowed to become sellers until the 1880s. The shop eventually closed in the 1990s.

Below: Townsend's Cycleries – 'all manner of cycles repaired'. Townsend's made their own bicycles and were in business for 100 years in Norfolk Street. The first bicycle was made and ridden in Cambridge in 1863. Early designs had wooden wheels and were called velocipedes. In 1868 a Cambridge blacksmith invented a 'suspension wheel' with thin iron spokes. By 1910 reports of bicycles becoming a nuisance began to appear in the newspapers. The reports called for bans in particular streets and complained of machines blocking the pavements and of professional thieves stealing bicycles and putting them on the train for London. Nearly 100 years later, the stories are still the same!

The Civic Restaurant was started in the early days of the Second World War as part of the Government's British Restaurant scheme to provide cheap meals for as many people as possible. It was originally situated in the Pitt Club in Jesus Lane but moved to Petty Cury, into the old post office building, which had also been used as the headquarters of the ARP and Special Constabulary. The restaurant remained there until 1972 (when this photograph was taken), sometimes cooking over 1,000 meals for customers and for the WRVS meals-on-wheels, until the area was redeveloped.

The Co-op store, Mill Road, 1908. The Co-operative Society was founded in 1868, when the wages of labourers averaged 11s per week; at the time, £1 or 20s was deemed a good wage, so the labourers' wages made life a constant struggle to survive. The original committee was made up of shoemakers, odd-job men, builder's labourers and carpenters, who banded together to trade co-operatively. The object of the society was to raise a fund by voluntary subscription to enable the purchase of food, fuel and clothing, which they sold to members with a dividend on purchases to help poor families afford necessities. They also supported educational projects for the working class. Several stores were opened, including the Mill Road store in 1908 and, later, the main store in Burleigh Street, where the new Robert Sayle building stands today.

Robert Sayle and Co. was founded in 1840, on a smaller site than the area recently vacated to make way for the Grand Arcade development. Robert Sayle, who lived over the store and was a philanthropist who was involved in the provision of gas lighting and the early development of the shopping centre of Cambridge, announced his intention in 1840 to 'sell linen drapery, silk mercery, hosiery, haberdashery and straw bonnets to the nobility, gentry and the inhabitants of the town'. The store joined the John Lewis group in 1940 and remains an enduring success story. A brand new shop is planned in the new Grand Arcade.

On a more modern note, the Swinging Sixties came to Cambridge here at the Alley Boutique in Post Office Terrace, where miniskirts and feather boas first made their appearance. Fashion really does go round in circles!

eight

Leisure

Cricket on Parker's Piece, 1900. Cricket has been played in Cambridge since the game's conception and still endures today on Parker's Piece, in the very centre of the city, despite worries over maintenance costs. The legendary Jack Hobbs played here and is immortalised in the Hobbs Pavilion, which still serves cooling drinks on a summer's day.

Trinity College servants, *c.* 1860. They may look light years away from their modern counterparts but win prizes for the sartorial elegance of their hats.

This was the very first university college servants' cricket XI to visit Oxford in 1865. Cambridge won by five wickets, with Oxford winning the return match by nine wickets.

Bowling taking place in 1950 on Christ's Pieces, another of Cambridge's popular green spaces, which remain the lungs of this traffic-polluted city. Bowling greens had been laid in the grounds of the Cambridge colleges in the seventeenth century, when the game was very popular. The Bowls Association was formed in Cambridge in 1927 and in 1930 the Cambridge and County Bowling Club began to meet.

Local children keeping cool at the paddling pool at Newnham in the hot summer of 1933, with no storm clouds on the horizon yet.

Bare-knuckle boxing in Newmarket Road, *c.* 1910. Unofficial bare-knuckle boxing bouts used to be held, but not under the strict rules laid out by the Marquis of Queensbury in the 1850s. They were often brutal and bloody, organised by unscrupulous promoters out to make a profit, whoever won. The venues were kept secret until the last minute, with details spread by word of mouth, and the audience was a mix of aristocratic and working men, with a few pickpockets thrown in. Often members of the judiciary enjoyed the spectacle too, although they should have stopped them happening. Some encounters were barbaric and could result in death, as they could go on for several hours, until one or other contestants collapsed. However, this bout looks like a less barbaric, featherweight version.

Members of the Cambridge University Bicycle Club with their penny-farthing racing machines. The man standing right of centre is possibly famous cyclist Ion Keith-Falconer.

Arthur George Markham, another famous cyclist, outside Great St Mary's church in 1905, embarking on a record-breaking 24-hour endurance ride in which he covered 307 miles.

Gonville Rovers football team, who met Comberton United in the first round of the Cambridgeshire Junior Cup and defeated them by two goals to nil in 1908. Cambridge is believed to have played a key part in football history, helping to set standard rules for the game. Early in the nineteenth century, each public school had its own set of rules, which posed a problem for Cambridge, who received students from Eton, Harrow, Rugby and Winchester.

Opposite above: Madingley Hall hunting party, 1910. This traditional pastime may soon pass into the history books. Madingley Hall is a Tudor mansion which was possibly built as a hunting lodge by John Hynde and later extended. The Hall was sold in 1905 to Colonel Thomas Harding, whose family had made 'new money' in the wool-combing trade in Leeds.

Opposite below: St John's College tennis courts in 1916.

Midsummer Fair, *c.* 1910. The fair has been held on Midsummer Common since 1209, when King John granted the charter giving permission for its inception. Except for the plague years of 1630, 1636 and 1637, when it was cancelled for fear of spreading infection, the fair has met every summer. Today it is a funfair but years ago it was the scene of the sale of goods, including pottery; it was called the Pot Fair in the eighteenth century. Food on sale at that time consisted of pease pudding, cockles and other seafood, nougat and gingerbread fairings in the shape of 'husbands and wives'. The gingerbread was wrapped in gilt paper, hence the phrase 'taking the gilt off the gingerbread'.

Steam yachts owned by Baker and Savage of King's Lynn at a Midsummer Fair, *c.* 1920. With the advent of steam, after 1870, fairground rides like these became very popular.

The Playhouse cinema stood on the corner of Mill Road and Covent Garden. It was built in 1912 and was Cambridge's first purpose-built cinema. It was demolished in the 1960s to make way for a supermarket. This was just one of several cinemas to be lost in Cambridge before the advent of the multiscreen. Here, Eddie Cantor is playing in *Kid Millions*.

The Victoria cinema in Market Hill opened in 1915 in the old Electric Theatre. By 1940 Cambridge had 7,400 regular cinema seats. This was the golden age of cinema and queues like this were commonplace. The Victoria closed in 1988.

The old Regal played host to many famous groups in the 1960s; these excited fans are at a Rolling Stones concert. According to a story in the local paper, elaborate plans to provide the group with a decoy car failed when two members of the group did not show up at the rendezvous on the outskirts of Cambridge, no doubt due to a heavy night beforehand. Recently when Bill Wyman was asked about the story, he could not remember it, which proves he really was a part of the sixties, for it is said that if you can remember the sixties, you weren't there!

These happy fans are posing with that other famous group who had a few hits! The Beatles came to the Regal in 1963. The Regal closed in 1997 and reopened as a fun pub and art cinema.

A student Rag Day parade, 1935. The students are having fun and raising money for charity. Today's rag escapades seem tame compared to some from the past, including placing an Austin Seven motor car on the roof of the Senate House in June 1958. The pranksters were thought to have used building equipment left nearby by workmen to hoist up the car, which fortunately did not contain an engine. Other past pranks include the painting of a false zebra crossing on the road at the top of St John's Street, Rag Day streakers, bed races, sponsored swims, punts on wheels, 'flying' into the Cam covered in flaming meths, bare-belly bank raids, mock funeral parades and even a beauty contest judged by Prince Charles in 1969.

Corpus Christi College students and guests in their finery for a ball. The May Balls, held in June, are a highlight of the university year, after all the hard work has been done.

May Day revels at the Central School for Girls in the 1920s. Here the May Queen is crowned in an eagerly awaited traditional ceremony. The intricate dances and simple songs would have been rehearsed for weeks and the school hall would be decorated with cowslips from Coldham's Lane for the ceremony.

Pupils from the Central School for Girls dancing around the maypole. The school is now Parkside Community College.

Good Friday Skipping on Parker's Piece, 1937. This local custom is steeped in folklore. Thought to have been a fertility rite to hasten the germination of the next season's crops, it was traditionally carried out by women but here both girls and boys seem to be having fun.

Cambridge volunteer fire brigade engine decorated for the coronation of Edward VII in 1902, with Captain Greef standing at the front.

Costermonger barrow race, Boxing Day 1913. This race is thought to have been run between Newmarket Road and Six Mile Bottom. The barrows would normally be used to transport goods from the station into town and would often be loaded with fruit and vegetables.

These somewhat bewildered-looking children have gathered for the proclamation of King George V on 10 May 1910 at Shire Hall, Cambridge.

nine

Work

Travelling scissor-grinder Levi Loveridge toured the area in the 1930s, sharpening knives and scissors. He was the father of sixteen children.

Lame Walter, who sold newspapers from his customised four-wheeled bicycle, at Jesus Green in the 1920s.

Opposite below: Two mobile sweeps from the company of J.R. Odell, 1909. In the days of coal fires, it was important to keep chimneys swept as, if left, they could catch fire, with disastrous consequences. At this time, the air would have been polluted by coal smoke from the factories, the gasworks and from thousands of home fires, creating a smoggy atmosphere.

Above: Scotland Road, 1920s. The horse-drawn milk cart delivered milk door to door in the days before milk was delivered in bottles. The old gas lamp in the foreground may have carried electricity for, when electricity was introduced, many of the old ornamental gas lamps were converted.

Above: Potts Brewery, Quayside, *c.* 1880. Quayside was Cambridge's main wharf; beer, barley and malt were all delivered here by barge. The firm of Potts was set up in the mid-1850s and had a large yard with buildings on all four sides, which have since been demolished. Billheads proudly proclaim HRH Prince of Wales (later Edward VII) as a patron, when he was an undergraduate at Cambridge. The business was sold in 1895 to the Star Brewery and the area is now the scene of café society, with many bars and restaurants.

Left: Fish-curer Arthur Jenkins of No. 23 Magdalene Street, 1909. He used to cure fish brought from the docks downriver to Quayside.

Foster's Mill, seen here in the 1920s, was situated beside the station, an area being developed at the moment. The mill was built in 1898 and modernised in 1950; it was originally owned by the Foster family, who were also bankers. The ornate Lloyds TSB Bank building on the corner of Hobson Street still bears the inscription 'Foster's Bank' over the main doorway. The mill was eventually taken over by Spillers, who milled local wheat to make flour for biscuits and cakes.

The instrument-making shop of the Cambridge Instrument Co., 1920. Originally called the Cambridge Scientific Instrument Co., or the Scientific, it was founded in 1881 by Horace Darwin, the youngest surviving son of Charles Darwin, the famous botanist. The firm manufactured scientific instruments for the rapidly expanding university scientific research departments, including the electrocardiograph, and later instruments for industry. The firm also did secret war work, manufacturing degaussing equipment, which neutralized the magnetisation of ships with an encircling current, as a precaution against magnetic mines.

Above: The Pye factory decorated for Christmas, 1955. In 1896 William Pye left the Cambridge Instrument Co. and set up his own company manufacturing scientific instruments. The company went on to manufacture and develop radio, TV, wartime radar and communications equipment, closed-circuit TV, broadcasting equipment, telephone equipment, public address and office intercoms, record players and even records. The company joined forces with Unicam, the company of another ex-Cambridge Scientific employee, Sidney Stubbens, to form Pye Unicam in 1934. Pye had several sites in Cambridge and was taken over by Philips in 1967.

The first post-war inspection of Cambridge Borough fire brigade took place in 1919. The first fire station was opened in 1901 in Burleigh Street; prior to this, fires would be fought by volunteer college crews and crews attached to insurance companies. The volunteer firemen used hose-reel carts, which drew water from the mains. They had no fire engine until 1906, when a steam fire engine was purchased as well as a smoke helmet linked by 95ft of hose to bellows so that the fireman could stand in smoke to put out fires. In 1920 a motor fire engine was purchased and in 1921 the police took over firefighting duties. By 1938 the Auxiliary Fire Service had became the National Fire Service and in 1964 the Parkside fire station was opened.

Opposite below: Women at work at the Cambridge Tapestry Co. in the 1930s. The company originally repaired valuable old tapestries but they are most famous for the Royal Jubilee tapestry made for Queen Mary and King George V and for the tapestry which hangs in Anglesey Abbey, which depicts the abbey and the surrounding villages as seen from the air.

The four Carter brothers were all members of the Borough police force in 1890. Policemen of the borough force, set up in 1836, were expected to be at least 5ft 7in tall and aged between twenty-one and forty. Each policeman had his own beat. Officers had to know all the streets, courts and houses and be able to recognise the inhabitants of each house on his beat. A typical beat took the officer along Petty Cury, down White Hart Yard to Black Ditch, up Falcon Street into Petty Cury again, across Market Hill, down Warwick Street, along St Mary's Passage, King's Parade and Benet Street to halfway up Free School Lane, then back to Benet Street, Peas Hill, around St Edward's church, along Union Street, Wheeler Street, part of Slaughterhouse Lane (Corn Exchange Street) and then back to the Town Hall to his post. This was repeated every half-hour!

Opposite below: By the 1930s motor vehicles were in use to collect the mail from pillar boxes around Cambridge and in 1934 a new head post office was built in St Andrew's Street.

Above: An early Royal Mail horse and trap. The first post office in Cambridge was situated in Green Street. The public were served through a small window, which looked out onto the pavement, on which people would tap for attention from the cashier inside. In 1885 the post office moved to the corner of Petty Cury, on the site of the old Wrestlers Inn. At this time, there were eleven town postmen and three college postmen and the mail was conveyed to the railway station by means of a horse-drawn mail van, formerly used as a hearse!

Left: A member of the railway staff at Cambridge station in the 1920s, with Foster's Mill in the background.

Below: Claud Hamilton locomotive No. 1861 of the Great Eastern Railway, *c.* 1917. The area had a proud tradition of railway workers, both in the steam days, when firemen worked hard to keep the fires stoked, and in the early days of diesel, before the swingeing Beeching cuts of the 1960s closed many stations.

Railway workers were one of the groups that participated in the General Strike of 1926, in support of the miners who were striking against wage cuts of between 10 per cent and 25 per cent, and against longer hours. Other groups which supported them were the transport workers, dockers, printers, builders, and iron and steel workers; a total of 3 million men came out on strike in May 1926. The strike lasted around ten days and, during this time, undergraduates, relishing the adventurous respite from revision for exams, were drafted in to deliver essential goods, despite coming under violent attack. The miners continued to strike until October, when hardship forced them back to work and they were compelled to accept less pay and longer hours. The City Arms in Sturton Street is the likely setting of this photograph, so these thirsty pickets may have stopped for a drink.

Workers from the Cambridge Electric Supply Co. installing a substation in Market Place, September 1898. St Mary's church can be seen in the background. The installation of electricity in central Cambridge caused much upheaval and interest in 1898.

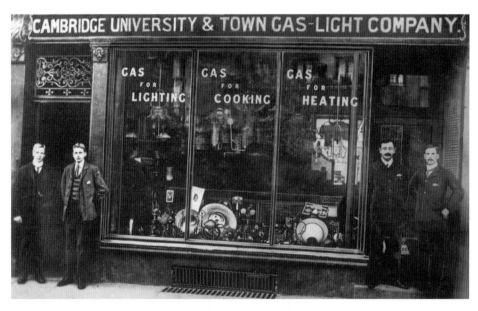

The premises of the Cambridge University and Town Gas-Light Co., No. 42 Sidney Street, 1908. Gas was introduced to Cambridge by John Grafton in 1826. Coal gas was used, after earlier experiments with oil had been unsuccessful. Cambridge had no large factories needing lighting but it had very dark streets and people were afraid of crime, either real or perceived. The Cambridge University and Town Gas-Light Co., which brought gas to Cambridge, was originally called the Cambridge Gas-Light Co. in the 1830s but changed its name in 1867.

The gasworks was built next to the river so that coal from the Yorkshire coal mines could be unloaded easily from the barges. This site remained in use for 170 years, until it was demolished to make way for a supermarket. The gas holder, which was erected in 1908 and was 90ft tall, was demolished in 1973.

Marshall of Cambridge was set up by Arthur Marshall with the support of his father, David, who, although originally a college servant, had been one of the first to see the potential of the motor car and built a business hiring cars to undergraduates. Arthur, as well as being a keen athlete who went to the Paris Olympics as a reserve in 1924, fell in love with flying. He bought a Gypsy Moth and established a flying school in 1929; by the end of the Second World War, 20,000 pilots had been trained there. The airport has since grown and the Marshall company has been involved in every British-built aircraft since the war; the droop nose of the Concorde was built there.

Other local titles published by Tempus

On Fenner's Sward
GILES PHILLIPS

Cambridge University Cricket Club is steeped in tradition. The first recorded game saw the Gentlemen of Cambridge take on the Gentlemen of Eton in 1755. The university has played a significant part in the history of cricket ever since. In all, Cambridge has produced nearly eighty Test players and twenty England captains. Beautifully illustrated, this is an essential read for anyone with an interest in the heritage of the great game.

0 7524 3412 8

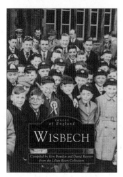

Ely Then & Now
PAMELA BLAKEMAN

The city of Ely has undergone great change in both its architecture and society within a relatively brief space of time over the last couple of centuries. This book provides an insight into the history of modern Ely and its people, and affords the reader a valuable opportunity for comparisons both then and now.

0 7524 2652 4

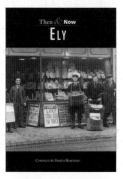

Wisbech
KIM BOWDEN AND DAVID RAYNER

This selection of over 200 old photographs of Wisbech illustrates some of the many changes that have occurred in the town during the first sixty years of the century. The pictures show how leisure and working activities have altered, sometimes dramatically, and illustrate the may changes that have taken place in the appearance of the streets and buildings of Wisbech.

0 7524 0740 6

Cambridge: The Hidden History
ALISON TAYLOR

By combining the results of archaeological excavation carried out over the last thirty years with important discoveries in previous centuries, Alison Taylor is able to piece together the history of Cambridge through prehistoric, Roman, Anglo-Saxon and medieval times, and then the expansion of the university in later centuries.

0 7524 1914 5

If you are interested in purchasing other books published by Tempus, or in case you have difficulty finding any Tempus books in your local bookshop, you can also place orders directly through our website

www.tempus-publishing.com